For D.R.

Each page is full of objects from the garage
which are used for different things.

ORCHARD BOOKS
96 Leonard Street, London EC2A 4RH
Orchard Books Australia
14 Mars Road, Lane Cove, NSW 2066
ISBN 1 85213 331 7 (hardback)
ISBN 1 85213 509 3 (paperback)
First published in Great Britain 1992
First paperback publication 1993
Copyright © Venice Shone 1992

The right of Venice Shone to be identified as the author and
illustrator of this work has been asserted by her in accordance
with the Copyright, Designs and Patents Act, 1988.
A CIP catalogue record for this book is available from the
British Library.
Printed in Belgium

Garage

VENICE SHONE

ORCHARD BOOKS

a garage full of objects

3

looking after the car

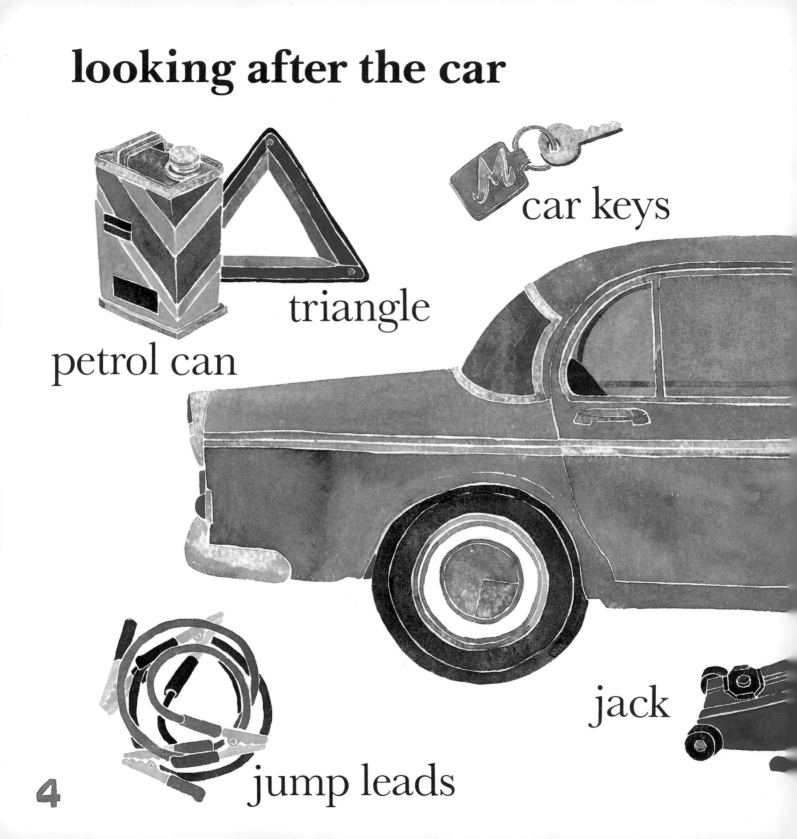

petrol can

triangle

car keys

jump leads

jack

4

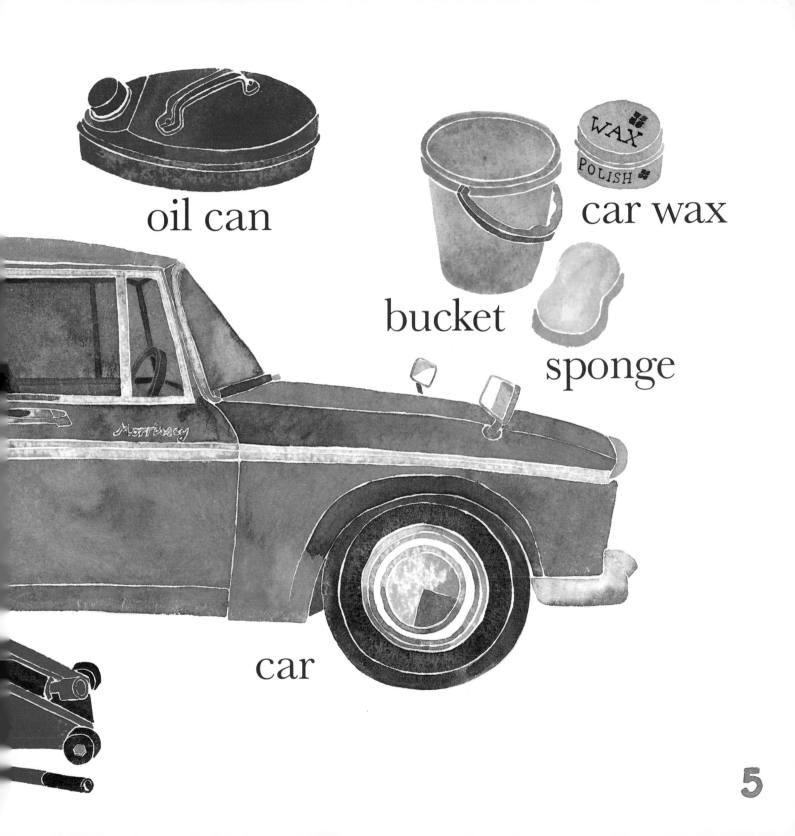

oil can

car wax

bucket

sponge

car

5

mending the bicycle

bicycle bag

saddle bag

bungee cord

bicycle lights

bicycle pump

cycling gloves

bicycle oil

spanner

puncture
repair kit

bicycle

painting

chair

white spirit

tin of paint

rag

paint brush

newspaper

8

child's bicycle

brush
and
paint

child's trolley

9

painting

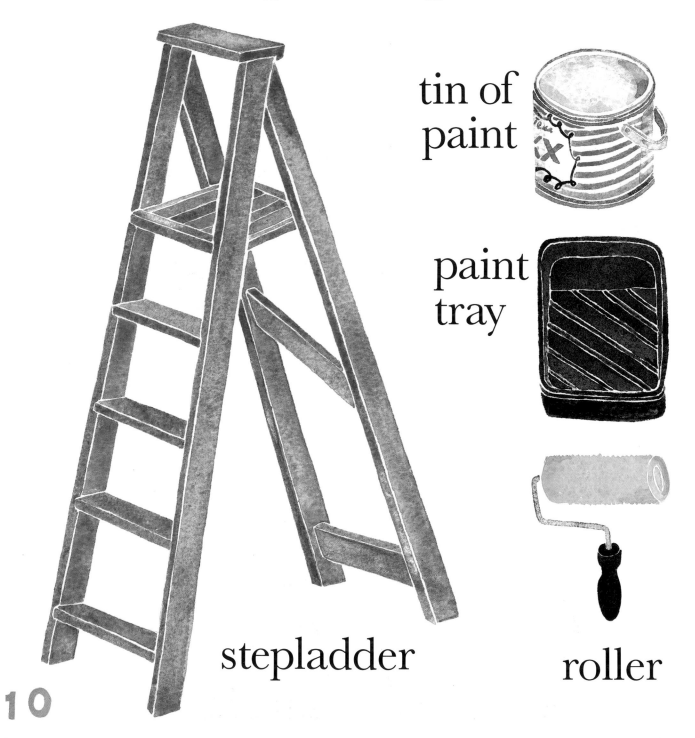

tin of
paint

paint
tray

stepladder

roller

10

lots of useful little things

box full of useful bits

mending and making

glue

saw

paint

G-cramp

paint brush

hammer

nails

12

workbench

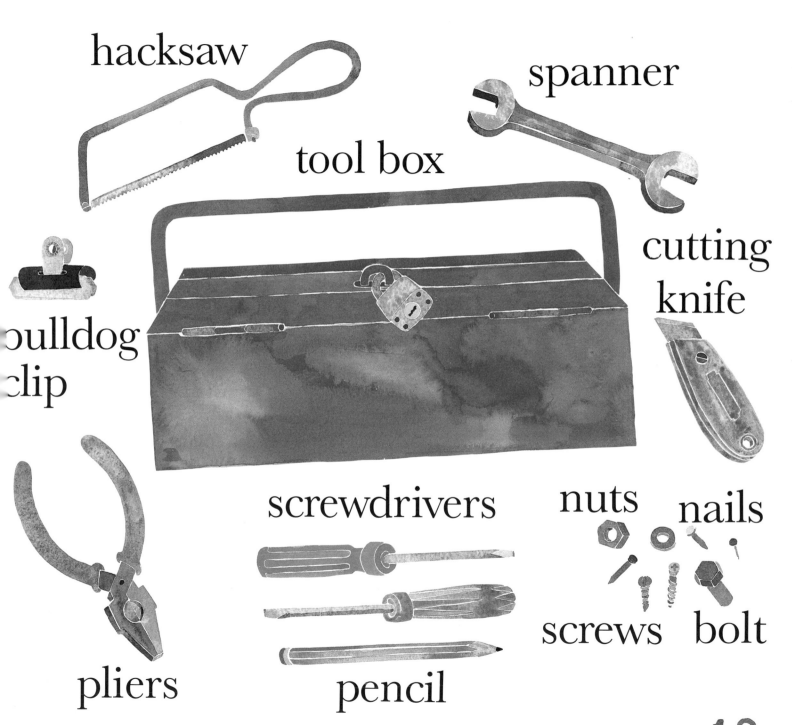

hacksaw

spanner

tool box

cutting
knife

bulldog
clip

screwdrivers

nuts

nails

pliers

screws

bolt

pencil

13

gardening things

fork

spade

hoe

rake

14

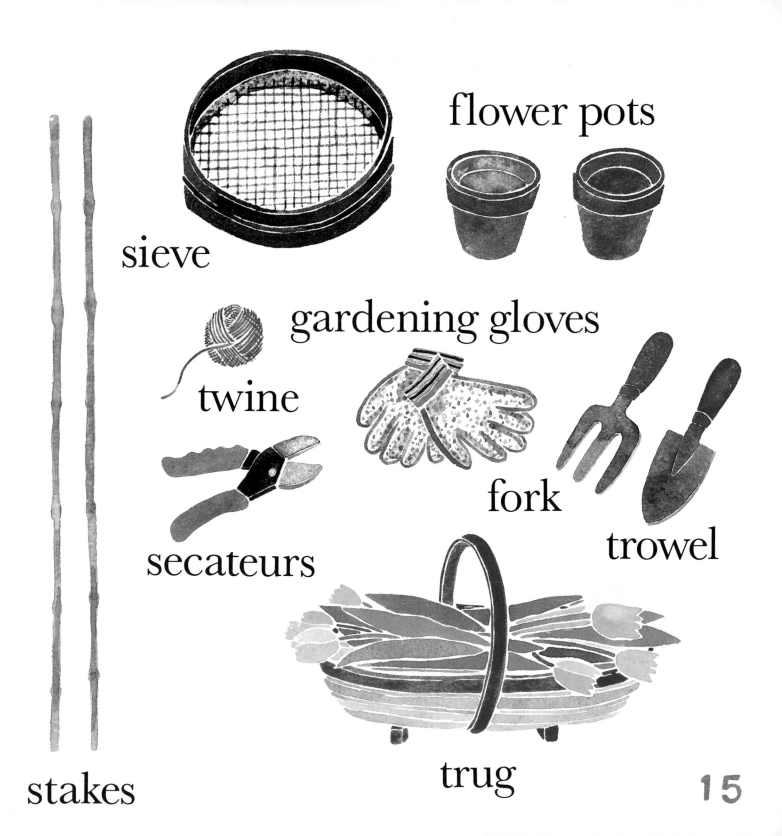

sieve

flower pots

twine

gardening gloves

secateurs

fork

trowel

stakes

trug

15

more garden tools

trellis

wheelbarrow

FERTILIZER

watering cans

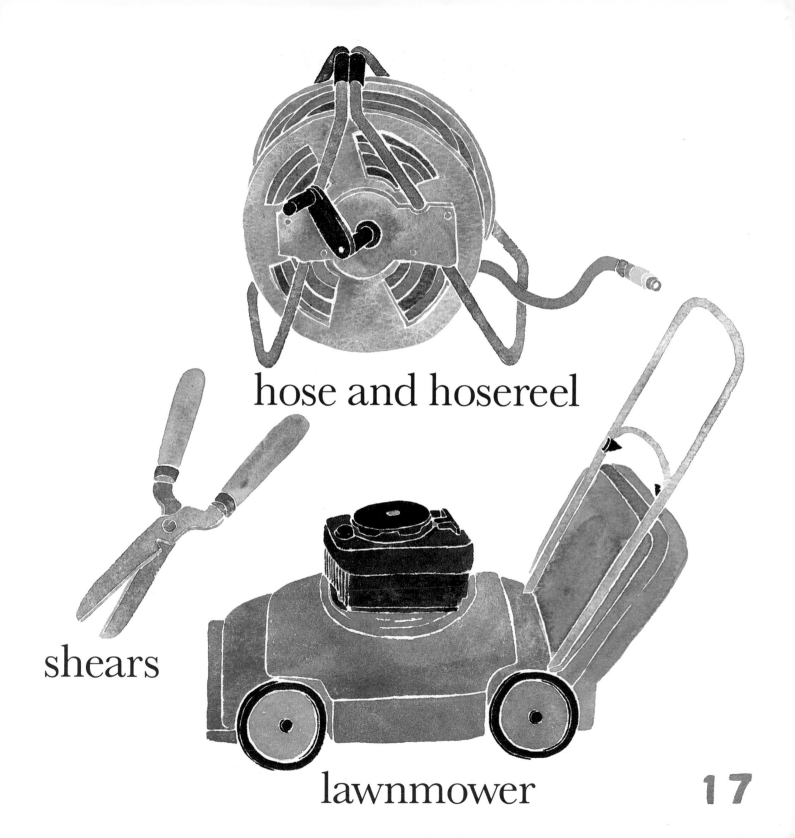

hose and hosereel

shears

lawnmower

17

for relaxing in the garden

parasol

deckchair

18

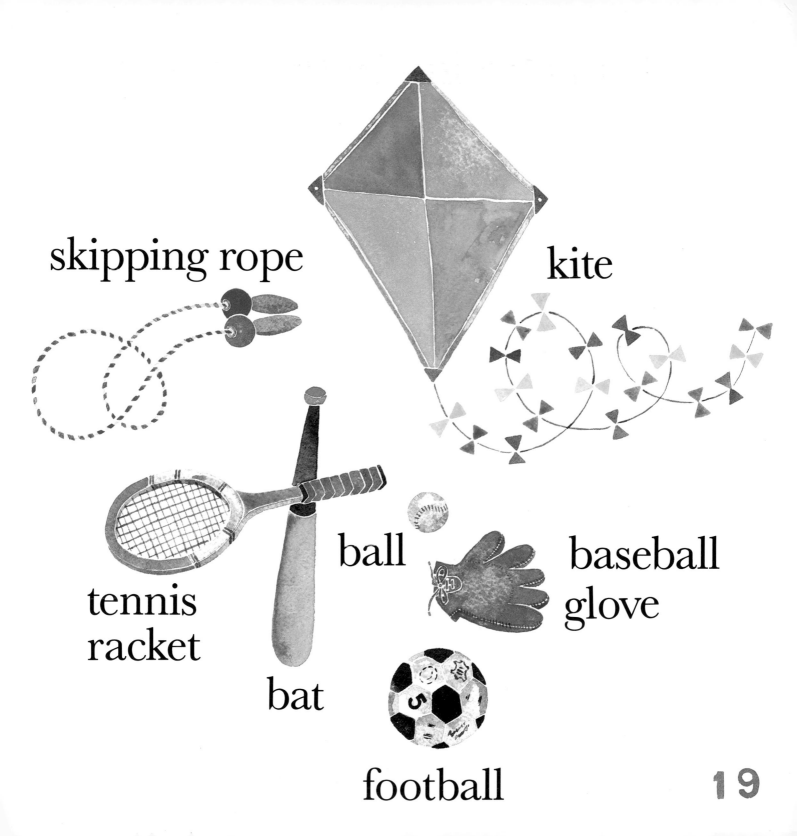

skipping rope

kite

tennis
racket

ball

bat

baseball
glove

football

19

holiday things

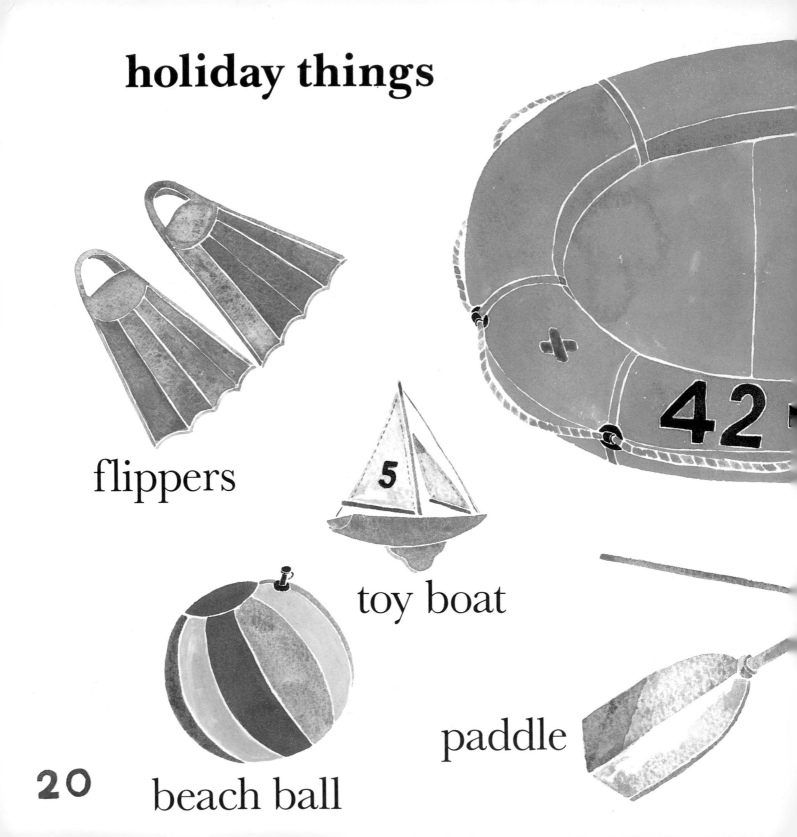

flippers

toy boat

5

42

beach ball

paddle

rubber dinghy

holiday shoes

mask

fishing net

bucket and spade

21

camping things

tent

fishing
basket

fishing rod

saucepan

camping stove

plate

kettle

mugs

baby mug

fishing umbrella

matches

camping stool

torch

23

things to be stored

COAL

dustbin

saw

log basket

24

basket of apples

POTATOES

onions

vegetable rack

dried flowers

bottles of wine

rubber boots

25